Authority of the Word

-A- Prayer for Rapid Transformation

Z.O.A OLADEJO.

Unless otherwise indicated,
All Scripture quotations are from
The King James Version of the Bible.

Authority of the Word
©
Oladejo Zipporah Omowunmi Adenike
ISBN-13: 9789789092406
ISBN-10: 9789092407

Published for:

The Lord's Portion Publishers
P.O.Box 6742, Ikeja, Lagos Nigeria.
Email: lordsportionmin@yahoo.com
Telephone: +234 9036995904, 803 473 9470,
0802 931 6302, 0807 577 5836,

By
Lozy-Lazz Nigeria Limited
Suite T 01 2nd floor, Alade Shopping Mall
Allen Avenue, Ikeja, Lagos.

All rights reserved under International Copyright Law. Contents and/or cover may not be reproduced in whole or in part in any form without the express written consent of the Author.
Printed in Nigeria. Sept 2010.

Dedication

This book is dedicated to the memory of my Dear Mother, MRS VICTORIA ADEDUUNI AKINWUNMI and everyone that is going through challenging moment in life. I have a hope that they shall soon be overcomers.

Acknowledgment

My heartfelt indebtedness goes to the Almighty God for His faithfulness in the successful completion of this book. My deepest appreciation also goes to my dear husband, Rev. Mobolaji Adeniyi Christopher Oladejo for his great contributions as regards the concept of this book. My gratitude to you is unquantifiable because without your input, this work would not have seen the Light of the day.

I also want to recognize the following people who assisted in the production of the manuscript. Mr Moses Akinleye Akinwunmi, my dear father, having someone like you is a priceless opportunity. Mr Abayomi Ajayi, and Deaconess Lawyer Bisi Ojuade. May God's desirable blessing constantly abide with you all and enrich your lives in Jesus name./

Contents

	Pages
Dedication	3
Acknowledgment	4
Introduction	7
Chapter 1: Authority of Light	11
Chapter 2: Authority of Expansion	22
Chapter 3: Authority of Water	30

Chapter 4:
Authority of Various Kinds   38

Chapter 5:
Authority of Separation   44

Chapter 6:
Authority of Abundance   49

Chapter 7:
Authority of Man   58

Chapter 8:
Authority of Reproduction   67

Conclusion   76

About the Author

Introduction

Authority of the Word *comprises* eight authoritative words that God used to create the Earth and *its content* (creation). The Bible says in the book of Genesis 1:2 that *"The earth was formless and empty, and darkness covered the deep waters. And the Spirit of God was hovering over the surface of the waters"*. Thus in the beginning, the earth was formless and darkness was upon the surface of the Earth, simply put, the Earth did not have any good meaning. This prompted God to speak the eight words of Authority at creation. That is the secret of the beauty the earth experienced afterwards. We can find an extensive account of these authoritative words in the first chapter of Genesis. Take a tour with me as we examine these words.

Authority of Light
Authority of Expansion
Authority of Water
Authority of Various Kinds
Authority of Abundance
Authority of Separation
Authority of Man
Authority of Reproduction

God's work in creation started by the pronouncement of these Words on the earth, which resulted in the glory and creation that begin to show forth. In the same vein, there are presently many people whose lives are in darkness and nothing meaningful can really be said about them. People go through different types of situation in life and even the forces of darkness have subjected many more into one form of bondage or the other. This is why a good number of people live lives characterized by emptiness.

Is your life empty or meaningless? Speak these authoritative words to your difficult situation and watch God do a perfect work in your life. There will definitely be a rapid and noticeable transformation in your life.

I have shared some of my experiences in this book, to challenge you and increase your faith, because with prayer, you can change that ugly state you presently find yourself. I urge you to go before the Lord in fasting for a period of seven days and taking each of these prayer points into your Spirit. Use them to address every area in your life that needs a change for the better. The Bible makes me understand in the book of Psalm 76:1 that *" In Judah is God known: his name is great in Israel."* Therefore, this book provides various inspirational and powerful songs that will take you to the realm of the Spirit, before you *begin* to pray. *Read the Bible passages before you go into the Lord's presence.* With a very strong conviction in me, I believe that as you begin to pray using each of these prayer points, your life will not remain the same in Jesus name. Every good change that you are expecting in your life will manifest in Jesus name.

Pastor ZOA Oladejo.

Let There Be Light

CHAPTER ONE

Authority of Light

God used the authority of Light on the first day of creation. (Genesis 1:2-5) "And the earth was without form, void; and darkness was upon the face of the deep. And the Spirit of God move upon the face of the water, and God said, Let there be light: and there was light And God saw the light, that it was good: and God divided the light from the darkness. And God called the light Day, and the darkness he called Night." And the evening and the morning were the first day".

It is no news that people experience dark moment everyday. I know of a 60 year old man who was blessed with the good things of life. He was the envy of all and sundry but when the moment of darkness visited him, he lost everything in one day. Even, young people are not spared of the vagaries of life. A young intelligent man I knew so well, graduated from the university with first class degree could not secure gainful employment ten years after graduation. This state of joblessness has made it impossible for him to achieve things in life because he is fixated at that point.

Do you think his case is pathetic? Here is yet another story. A young man I am acquainted with got a job in a reputable company after graduation from the university. He was so brilliant that his colleagues looked up to him for inspiration, because to them, he was a model. Unfortunately, this young man with a very promising future suddenly took ill and was mistakenly injected with wrong drugs in the course of his treatment. This once vibrant young man was rendered useless and had to be locked up somewhere. Today, the devil afflicts people with different types of diseases that cannot be explained medically.

The Bible says in Ephesians 6:12 that *"For we wrestle not against flesh and blood, but against principalities, against powers, against the rulers of the darkness of this world, against spiritual wickedness in high places"*. Sometime ago, precisely about two years into my marriage, I went through a very challenging moment of darkness. I unexpectedly became very sick and everything in my life stood still. Initially, I thought it was just malaria or fever, which would go over time, but the sickness persisted. I was taken from one hospital to another, and different doctors treated me to no avail. Several medical examinations were carried out with thousands of naira, but medically, i was certified okay. Every day I was getting weaker and it seemed my life was coming to an end. My home was turned upside down, I lost my job in the process and I was

The power of the Holy Spirit is usually released whenever we speak the word of authority.

becoming an object of ridicule even within the ministry. In actual fact, everyone around me lost hope because they didn't really understand what was going on. This was really a very dark moment in my life. Beloved, six months into this challenge, after series of persistent prayers from men and women of God, the dark period began to roll away and my health was restored.

I don't know what dark situation you are presently going through, but I know a GOD that has the authority of light. He alone will speak light into the dark situation of your life. Break the grip of the devil over your life. God's authoritative word will speak light into every of the dark area of your life in Jesus name.

The power of the Holy Spirit is usually released whenever we speak the word of authority. When there was nothing but darkness, confusion, God said *"let there be light and there was light* (Gen. 1:3.)" The Earth brought forth its glory and became meaningful.

Begin now, by speaking the word of light into all dark situations in your life.

Song:
O lord my God, when I in awesome wonder,
Consider all the works Thy hands have made,
I see the stars, I hear the rolling/mighty thunders,
Thy power throughout the universe displayed!

Chorus:
Then sings my soul, my Savior God, to Thee:
How great Thou art, how great Thou art!
Then sings my soul, my Savior God, to Thee:
How great Thou art, how great Thou art!

Prayer Points:
I speak the authority of Light that makes all things meaningful, into my life in Jesus name.
- **II Samuel 22:29**

"And God said, let there be light, and there was light", therefore, every good thing that is missing in my life, Light from heaven locate it for me in Jesus name
   - Genesis 1:3.

From today onward, I declare that any darkness covering me, be gone in Jesus name.
   -- II Samuel 22:29.

Darkness destroyed the initial glory of the earth, but You, O God turned it around! Arise as glory upon the issues of my life and let my life bring forth glory.
   -Genesis 1:3.

Every power of darkness covering my glory, and not allowing my glory to shine at the right time, authority of light destroy it in Jesus name.
   - John 1:5.

Lord, send the authority of light that caused a good change in the earth to my being in Jesus name.. —
Genesis 1:4.

Every power of darkness controlling the treasure of my life, fire of the Holy Spirit consume it in Jesus name.
- **Ephesians 6:12.**

Any darkness that is not allowing me to witness good things in my life, Father let your authority of light shine into it in Jesus name.
- **John 1:5.**

Father! pull my life out of every confusion that I've found myself in.
- **Job 12:22.**

Every glory of my life that my enemy has covered with darkness, Lord, pull my life out of it in Jesus name. - **Psalms 107:14.**

Every power of darkness killing my glory with words, Father, let their words over my life be destroyed in Jesus name.
- **Colossians 1:13.**

El- Gibor! (The great helper), you who helped the earth and delivered it from darkness and confusion, Help my life and deliver me in totality.
Genesis1:17-18.

Every vain labour or struggle that darkness is using as an instrument of bondage to hold my life, Lord, use the authority of light to deliver me in totality.
- **I Samuel 2:9.**

All those bargaining for my life in the dark market, Father, before the end of this year, destroy them in Jesus name
-**Psalms 27:1.**

God of the Host of Heaven, for my sake, enter into the dark market places and disorganize them in Jesus name.
- **Daniel 8:10.**

All those from the dark shooting at my life with arrow of limitation amidst my peer group, Father, blind them with sickness in Jesus name.
- **II Samuel 22: 15.**

You woman of the dark world that is throwing the stones of sorrow at my destiny, Lord, send back her stones of sorrow in Jesus name.
Psalm 18: 4.

Lord, use your word of authority redeem my glory from any power of darkness that has my Glory.
Leviticus 25:41.

Lord, every dark situation that has gone ahead of me this year, let your light shine upon it, that I may pass over it in Jesus name.
   -**Matthew 4:16.**

Julius (a custodian), Lord, deliver my life from every custodian of darkness that has the custody of my life.
   - **Acts 27:1.**

Every hand of darkness standing as an obstacle on my path and causing my struggles to multiply, Lord, cut it down with your sword.
   - **Hebrews 10:39.**

Every representative of darkness in custody of my life, Lord, release my destiny from their hands with your power in Jesus name.
   -**Esther 2: 3.**

Every custodian of darkness over my life, hear the word of the Lord "It shall not be well for the wicked", therefore, Lord, make their ways crooked! In Jesus name
- **Ecclesiastes 8:13.**

Every level of life that those with the power of darkness have said that I will not attain in life, Lord, take me there in Jesus name.
- **Genesis 12:1, 7.**

Every good thing missing in my destiny, light from Heaven, locate it for me in Jesus name.
- **Genesis 1:31.**

God wants you to expand

CHAPTER TWO

Authority of Expansion

Authority of Expansion is the second authoritative word God spoke at creation. The Bible says in Genesis 1: 6-8 "And *God said, let there be a firmament in the midst of the waters, and let it divide the waters from the waters. And God made the firmament, and divided the waters which were under the firmament from the waters which were above the firmament: and it was so. And God called the firmament Heaven. And the evening and the morning were the second day."*

The power of limitation has kept many people from enjoying God's plan for their lives. God's desire for us is expansion and not limitation. But many of us are stagnant. For example, I heard of some people who couldn't be promoted at work and remained at a particular level for many years because out of wickedness, someone hid their files.

Whereas for others who embarked on a business do not make progress after many years of toiling. Companies that were incorporated are not doing well and many others start folding up.

The second thing God did was to speak to the firmament. He made the firmament and divided the waters. In II Kings 6:1-2, the Bible says *"And the sons of the prophets said unto Elisha, Behold now, the place where we dwell with thee is too strait for us. Let us go, we pray thee, unto Jordan, and take thence every man a beam, and let us make us a place there, where we may dwell. And he answered, Go ye".* The sons of prophet who were willing and devoted to spreading the word of God, asked for permission from Elijah so they could construct a bigger place to accommodate them. God wants us to expand and not be in the same position throughout our life time here on earth.

Many in positions of authority use their position wrongly. Some would even swear that no one under them will grow or expand.

Sometime ago, I was employed as a System Analyst Programmer with an Insurance company in Lagos, and for about eight years in that organization, my career was at a standstill. I later realized that my manager felt threatened by my potentials and qualifications that he hid my file. He didn't recommend me for promotion for over eight years. Other members of staff in other departments, lower in grade than me were promoted based on their manager's recommendation. But my case was different until I took my case to the Almighty God. During this period in my life, I was frustrated, depressed, and I would cry several times to the Lord to help me from that experience.

Does this sound like your story? Have faith in God that the same God that came to my rescue is still here and will bring about the required expansion in your life. Do not be discouraged and be hopeless. God told Abraham in Genesis 13: 15 *"For all the land which thou seest, to thee will I give it, and to thy seed forever."* Also in Genesis 15:18 He said *"In the same day the LORD made a covenant with Abram, saying, Unto thy seed have I given this land, from the river of Egypt unto the great river, the river Euphrates".* Go before the Lord and speak the authoritative word of expansion to your stagnant situations. Your career, business, home and every area of your endeavor will expand in Jesus name. Begin now by speaking these words of expansions into every stagnant situation in your life.

Song:
>Who is like unto Thee, O Lord /2ce
>Among the gods?
>Who is like Thee?
>Glorious in holiness
>Fearful in praises
>doing wonders, halleluyah.

God wants us to expand and not be limited.

Song:
>Oh Lord my God,
>how excellent is your name
>In all the earth,
>how excellent is your name.

Prayer Point
>El- Gibor!, my life has been limited!, Lord! speak the word of expansion into my life, that I may be delivered from my limitations.
>
>**Genesis 1:6**

Lord! By now I should have been at the top of my career, speak the authority of expansion into my life that I may be at the top of my career in Jesus name.
Genesis 9: 27.

God! Touch the mind of the person tying down my blessing and cause him to release it in Jesus name.
Genesis 41: 40 - 41.

Whoever is in position of authority that is in custody of my blessing and the glory of my job, Father cause him to release it in Jesus name.
Genesis 39:4.

Where has my blessing been hidden? . In whose custody is my blessing? Host of heaven, use the authority of the word to release my blessing from such a person in Jesus name.
Genesis 27:35.

Father, let the power of authority in you that made the firmament (Expansion) make my expansion come quickly in Jesus name. **Genesis 1: 7.**

Lord, at my place of work and amidst my peer group, make me the one to be sought after.
Romans 8:19.

Lord! Deliver me from every battle of struggling in Jesus name.
Psalm 34:10.

O God! Enlarge my coast like that of Jabez.
I chronicles 4:10.

Every family curse placing limitation on my life and destiny, fail in Jesus name.

Every evil hand destroying my life, catch fire In Jesus name..

God created water for existence

CHAPTER THREE
Authority of Water

"And God said, Let the waters under the heaven be gathered together unto one place, and let the dry land appear: and it was so. And God called the dry land Earth; and the gathering together of the waters called he Seas: and God saw that it was good". Genesis 1: 9-10.

The Bible says in Genesis chapter 2:5-6 *"And every plant of the field before it was in the earth, and every herb of the field before it grew: for the LORD God had not caused it to rain upon the earth, and there was not a man to till the ground. But there went up a mist from the earth, and watered the whole face of the ground."* The earth was not producing fruits because there was no rain. Here rain was the link between earth and heaven.

Therefore, for our lives to show forth glory, we need God to water our lives. The importance of water to existence is not hidden. In our day to day existence, we know the value of water as a result of lots of things that we do with it. We drink water, use it to cook, wash clothes, bath and do many other tasks that are essential for our daily living. Plants cannot grow without water and animals will die without water. According to experts, the human body cannot survive without water longer than three days. Water is very important! Thus as children of God, for our lives to radiate God's glory, we need to be well watered with the power of God.

Whenever you see a garden that is well watered, it flourishes and radiates beauty; that is how we are supposed to be. We are to radiate God's glory at all times. Pathetically, because of the economic meltdown and situations in the world today, many families are not flourishing but are encountering dry times. Dry times arise as a result of retrenchment, joblessness, poverty, stagnation, famine and diverse types of lack.

These days, many struggle through life to get the Little they have, while others struggle in vain with nothing to show. This is not the plan of God for our lives. The Bible says in Psalms 72:7 *"In his days shall the righteous flourish; and abundance of peace so long as the moon endureth."* and in Psalms 72:16 *"There shall be an handful of corn in the earth upon the top of the mountains; the fruit thereof shall shake like Lebanon: and they of the city shall flourish like grass of the earth."* God's desire is that His children flourish and are blessed. The Bible says in Psalms 92: 12-14 *" The righteous shall flourish like the palm tree: he shall grow like a cedar in Lebanon. Those that be planted in the house of the LORD shall flourish in the courts of our God. They shall still bring forth fruit in old age; they shall be fat and flourishing;"*

Is your life dry? Prior to the global economic meltdown, were things well with you but right now, you are going through a dry period in your life and family? Speak the authoritative words below and experience God's glory in Jesus name.

Song One:

(1) There's not a friend like the lowly Jesus,
   No, not one! No, not one!
   None else could heal all our soul's diseases,
   No, not one! No, not one!
Chorus:
   Jesus knows all about our struggles,
   He will guide till the day is done;
   There's not a friend like the lowly Jesus,
   No, not one! No, not one!

(2) No friend like Him is so high and holy
   No, not one! No, not one!
   And yet no friend is so meek and lowly
   No, not one! No, not one!
   Chorus
(3) Never a gift like the Savior given
   No, not one! No, not one!
   Will He refuse saints a home in heaven?
   No, not one! No, not one!
   Chorus:

Song Two:

Let Your living water flow over my soul
Let Your Holy Spirit come and take control
Of every situation that has troubled my mind
All my cares and burdens on to You I roll

Chorus:
Jesus, Jesus, Jesus
Father, Father, Father
Spirit, Spirit, Spirit

Come now, Holy Spirit, and take control
Hold me in Your loving arms and make me whole
Wipe away all doubt and fear and take my pride
Draw me to Your love and keep me by Your side

Chorus:
Jesus, Jesus, Jesus
Father, Father, Father
Spirit, Spirit, Spir

Prayer Points

Your word says that in the sweat of my face I shall eat bread; Jehovah Jireh! Water my job and every of my seed of sweat, Do not allow me to sow my seed of sweat in vain in the name of Jesus.
    Genesis 3:19.

Every water of bitterness that my destiny is drinking in abundance, Jesus, replace it with your water of life.
    Isaiah 30: 20, John 7:38.

Every water of the wicked ones that my destiny has drunk from in my sleep disrupting my journey in life, dry up in Jesus name.
    Mark 9:22.

The root that does not touch water cannot produce fruit, Father, let the root of my life touch water for it to bear fruits in the name of Jesus.
    II kings 19: 30.

Every axe of darkness that is standing between my root and water, break in Jesus name.
Matthew 3:10.

Lord! The earth did not have meaning until it rained, send into my life the power that will give my life a good meaning.
Genesis 2:5.

Lord! Release my life from every dryness and let the dew of heaven release blessings into my life in the name of Jesus.
Luke 4: 25, 26.

Lord! Turn my wilderness to greener pasture in Jesus name.
Psalm 23:2.

Rain on my seed of sweat that I may have the increase and fat of the earth.
Isaiah 30:23.

God Ordains Varieties

CHAPTER FOUR
Authority Of Various Kinds

The Bible says in Genesis 1: 11 - 13, " *And God said, Let the earth bring forth grass, the herb yielding seed, and the fruit tree yielding fruit after his kind, whose seed is in itself, upon the earth: and it was so. And the earth brought forth grass, and herb yielding seed after his kind, and the tree yielding fruit, whose seed was in itself, after his kind: and God saw that it was good. And the evening and the morning were the third day".*

Our lives deserve variety of blessings such as children, houses, cars, visa, good health, healing, promotions, increase, employment and so on. Who says you cannot have all these blessings in your life too? You can speak various kinds of blessings into your life with the authority of the word.

After God spoke light into the darkness that I Battled with just after my wedding, He began to speak various blessings into my Life. In fact, in the first month of my recovery, I became pregnant and a lot of people wondered how I would be able to carry through with the pregnancy knowing how bad my health had been in the past months. But Alas!, I did with God's grace, because, God was beginning to deposit various blessings in my life, and certainly the devil knew it. Two months after the delivery of my baby, I was called for an interview in one of the biggest Information Technology Companies in Lagos, Nigeria. In fact, I had to take my baby to the venue of the interview, because I was still breast feeding her. While I was facing the panel of interviewers, my husband was downstairs attending to the baby till I was through. Eight months into this job, I got another bigger job opportunity with several other blessings like international travels, a brand new car, new house and many others.

You may be wondering if you will ever be blessed with these beauties of life, I bet you, If you can only speak the word of authority of different kinds of blessings into your life, all your blessings across the four corners of the world will locate you in Jesus name. The time to speak the word is `now, so start speaking the authority of different kinds of blessings given below.

Song:
Father, do something new in my life/2ce
Something new in my life, Jesus
Do something new in my life / 2ce
Something new in my life Jesus.
Do something marvelous in my life /2ce
Something marvelous in my life, Amen.

Prayer Points

The Bible says that *"Lord you are the lifter of my head"*, the authority that lifts a person to a high place, enter my destiny today in Jesus name.
    Psalms 3:3.

The authority that lifts one to a higher level in life, that will make the world marvel; heaven send it into my destiny in Jesus name.
Matthew 9:8.

Lord! I have been tied with words of men and my blessing and glory have been bound, in the name of Jesus, authority of various kinds release variety of blessings into my life.
Isaiah 49:24-25.

Every angel that is supposed to deliver my blessings to me, do not refuse in Jesus name.
Luke 1:19.

The Bible says *"Lord, You are the lifter of my head"* Lord! from today onward, I receive my lifting in Jesus name.
Psalms 3:3.

Where people are talking about a casting down, I speak the authority of various kinds that will bring me promotions and lifting in Jesus name. **Psalms 75:6-7.**

The dead cannot see wonders, Lord as much as am living, make me see wonders in the land of the living.
Psalm 88: 10.

Authority of various kinds of blessings that my destiny is waiting for that will make my life good, Lord release it into my life.
Genesis 1:11.

Lord, bless me with abundant blessings among men and women.
Genesis 12:2.

Lord! Speak into my life the authority of various kinds of blessings
Ephesians 3:20.

God wants us separated from anything anti-glorious

CHAPTER FIVE

Authority Of Separation

The Bible says in Genesis 1:14-15 "And God said, *"Let there be lights in the expanse of the sky to separate the day from the night, and let them serve as signs to mark seasons and days and years, and let them be lights in the expanse of the sky to give light on the earth."* And it was so.

For God's glory to be seen in our lives, we need to separate ourselves from things that prevent God's glory from showing forth in our lives. We need to separate ourselves from sin and things that are not of God. The Bible says in the book of Romans chapter 6:1: *"What shall we say then? Shall we continue in sin, that grace may abound?"*.

Break ties with bad friends that can influence you negatively. Also, we have to do away with traits in us like spirit of timidity, fear, lack of confidence, hatred, anger, pride, because they can prevent God's glory in our lives. Speak the word of separation now into your life to separate you from things that will hinder God's Glory in your Life.

Song:
Our Lord God, Thou hast made the heavens and the earth by Thy great power;
Our Lord God, Thou hast made the heavens and the earth by Thine outstretched arm.

Chorus:
Nothing is too difficult for Thee
Nothing is too difficult for Thee
Great and mighty God,
Great in power and mighty in deeds,
Nothing, nothing, absolutely nothing,
Nothing is too difficult for Thee.

We need to separate ourselves from sin and things that are not of God.

Prayer Points:

Lord, speak the authority of separation to separate me and my short coming is taking the place of my glory.
Genesis 1: 14

Lord, speak separation between me and my time of weeping, sickness and vain labour.
Isaiah 65:19.

Every spirit that is wasting my season and time, in the journey of my life, authority of separation, separate us in Jesus name.
II Corinthians 6:17.

Every spirit of emptiness that is destroying my life gradually, Lord! separate us in Jesus name.
Nahum 2:10.

Authority of separation, separate me from every

spirit of debt, failure and hatred that are destroying the journey of my life.
Romans 8:35.

Every voice of man and opposition that needs to give way for my blessing to flow abundantly, Lord, separate them for my life
Job 38:25.

Lord, separate me from every spirit that is against my becoming influential in life.
Genesis 9:27.

God wants us to live in abundance.

CHAPTER SIX

Authority Of Abundance

The Bible says in the book of Genesis chapter 1: 20-23 *"And God created great whales, and every living creature that moveth, which the waters brought forth abundantly, after their kind, and every winged fowl after his kind: and God saw that it was good. And God blessed them, saying, Be fruitful, and multiply, and fill the waters in the seas, and let fowl multiply in the earth. And the evening and the morning were the fifth day.*

God wants us to live in abundance. The Bible says in the book of Ephesians 3:20 *"Now unto him that is able to do exceeding abundantly above all that we ask or think, according to the power that worketh in us".*

Also the book of III John 2 say *"Beloved, I wish above all things that thou mayest prosper and be in health, even as thy soul prospereth".*

However, what do we see happening today? People do not have enough not to even talk of having in abundance. When I was a little girl, my parents did ask us (my siblings and I) then as kids after each meal whether or not we were okay and if we were not, more food would be given to us.

But nowadays the majority of parents can even afford to feed their children three times daily, because the food in the house is not enough, and the one that is available needs to be adequately managed. Some parents do not have enough money to send their children to school. These days, parents pay lots of money as school fees for their children in private primary and tertiary institutions, and often times, struggle to make ends meet. This has become inevitable since public schools are ill-equiped and poorly financed.

The aged too are affected as they are being left uncared for, because their children do not have enough at their disposal. Towns, Countries in Africa and other developing countries around the world are living in abject poverty.

This is not the desire of God for our lives. As we have read in the scriptures, God wants us to have in abundance. Speak the authority of abundance into your life and experience the abundance of God. Begin now by speaking the authority of abundance of God's blessings.

Song:
God will make a way
Where there seems to be no way
He works in ways we cannot see
He will make a way for me
He will be my guide
Hold me closely to His side
With love and strength for each new day
He will make a way
He will make a way

Song:

There shall be showers of blessing:
This is the promise of love;
There shall be seasons refreshing,
Sent from the Savior above.

Chorus:
Showers of blessing,
Showers of blessing we need:
Mercy-drops round us are falling,
But for the showers we plead.

Prayer Points
Lord! Speak into my life, a source that will not dry up.
    Matthew 15: 37.

The glory of my life that is in the hand of someone I don't know, God of acceleration bring it forth to me.
    Genesis 44:1.

Every challenge weighing my destiny down not allowing me to become what I'm supposed to be, be destroyed in Jesus name.
Mark 2:21.

As fire removes the skin of a goat, fire of God, remove the garments of poverty from my life in Jesus name.
Proverb 11:24.

Everywhere that I've not been able to get to because of the challenges of my life, Lord! Take me there by your mercy.
Romans 9:15.

Lord Jesus! Reveal yourself in the journey of my life, that my life may not be empty.
Deuteronomy 29:29.

Every power that wants to turn my life into an empty vessel, Lord! Repay it with shame.
Psalm 6:10.

Lord! Every glory, that my destiny is awaiting, let it come upon me suddenly.
   Act 2:2.

The net of my life, catch lots of blessings in Jesus name.
   Luke 5:6.

The net of my life, do not break or leak again in Jesus name.
   Mark 1:19.

The net of my life, from today onward, begin to catch lots of blessings in Jesus name.
   John 21:6.

Lord! Put my destiny into great glory for others to see.
   Luke 21:27.

Lord, reward the work of my hand, do not allow me to sweat in vain.
   Genesis 3:19.

Lord, put an end to every waste in my life.
Isaiah 19:5.

Lord! Deliver me from ever fruitless and vain effort.
I Corinthians 15:58.

Lord, reveal to me today, every meaningful area of my life.
II Kings 6:6.

Lord! Locate and recover for me everything that has been stolen from my life that will give my life a good meaning.
I Kings 6:6.

God take me into the treasure of the Snow.
Job 38:22.

Lord, add to my source in all ways in the name of Jesus.
Hebrew 6:14.

As long as I live without sin, Father, whenever I lift my voice concerning a thing, allow abundance in Jesus name.
Job 38:29.

Lord, take me out of my limitation.
Psalms 78:41.

Lord, grant unto me the blessing of abundance that I will use to bless my generation.
Genesis 12:2.

Lord, the hand that you used in opening the door of today, use it to pave way for me not to labour in vain.
I Corinthians 15:58.

Every load that the wicked one has put on the journey of my life that is making me to labour in vain, Lord!, remove it in Jesus name.
Galatians 4:11.

God gave man authority to be in-charge

CHAPTER SEVEN

Authority Of Man

The Bible says in Genesis 1:26; 31 *"And God said, Let us make man in our image, after our likeness: and let them have dominion over the fish of the sea, and over the fowl of the air, and over the cattle, and over all the earth, and over every creeping thing that creepeth upon the earth. And God saw every thing that he had made, and, behold, it was very good. And the evening and the morning were the sixth day.*

Authority of Man is the authoritative word that God used to create man on the sixth day of creation. You need this authoritative word in your life too to show forth God's glory. I have realized that on our journey to success, we need people, (MAN). The Bible says in Genesis 2:5 " 5*And every plant of the field before it was in the earth, and every herb of the field before it grew: for the LORD God had not caused it to rain upon the earth, and there was not a man to till the ground.*

According to that scripture, the earth was meaningless because there was no rain and also importantly, because there was no man to till the ground. We all need "Man", and by this, I mean connection, on our way to the top and in life in general.

We need to pray that God to connects us with the right people (MAN) who will do our lives well. From my experience, the role that 'MAN' plays in our journey to success is very important. Man can make you and man can mar you. There are two scenarios in my own case that I would love to share with you to help you understand these prayers better.

On our journey to success, we need people

When God began to bless me with those different blessings like I noted earlier, at the Information Technology Company, I met a man there, who was the head of Administration. This man had some little Information Technology ideas and based on this knowledge, he did all within his power to bring me down and frustrate me because he felt that I was a threat to him. Several times on getting home after work, the first thing that I would discuss with people was the frustrations and blackmails at my work place. On some occasions at the office, tears would rolled down my cheeks and I was beginning to get tired of the environment again. But I refused to be tired because, I knew that God's blessings had started something good in me after my initial dark experiences. So, while all the blackmails was going on, I was taking many certification examinations and ignoring all the dangerous job politics the man was playing with me. To the glory of God, I passed some of these certification examinations which later helped me some months thereafter.

Some couple of months later, another man, in another organization, called my husband on the telephone to inform him that some expatriates, all the way from Kuwait, were in Nigeria looking for people with degrees and certification in Information Technology, and that I should call their number to tell them about myself. I did what I was told to do and was later invited for an interview the next day. I performed well in that interview and Alas! The door of international job opened for me through a phone call, I earn dollars in my own country. What a miracle! All these happened within one and a half years after the darkness I experienced when I was almost losing my life. Beloved, I tell you, our God is the same yesterday, today, and forever. I pray that God will link you up with the man who will connect you to your blessings in Jesus name. Take these prayer points and speak the authority of man into your life.

Song One:
Covenant keeping God,
there is no one like you,
Alpha & omega,
there is no one like you.

Song Two:
Oh Lord, You deserved the glory! 2ce
You rule on earth, as you reign in Heaven,
Oh Lord, you deserve the glory.
    - *Rev Mac Oladejo.*

Prayer Points:
Every law of man that has turned me to an

object of bondage for the wicked one, Lord cancel it in Jesus name.
Isa 49 : 24, 25.

Lord, you used the word and man to deliver Lazarus, use them to deliver me in Jesus name.
Isa 49:44.

Every word of men spoken to my life that is troubling me, cease in Jesus name.
Lamentations 4:37.

Father, destroy every reign of pain in my life, on my job and in my family.
Psalms 25:18.

Everything you have created through soil that is preventing my joy, Lord silence it today in Jesus name.
Genesis 1:12.

Every power of man and of the wicked controlling the day of my blessing, Lord clear

them in Jesus name.
Job 38:28.

O God, the good that a man cannot do for me, do it for me by your mercy.
Psalms 34:10.

Lord, replace with good people, every bad person that surrounds my life, causing issues of my life to be disrupted every day.
John 5:11, 12.

Lord for every man that wishes me pleasantries in my presence, but is destroying me in my absence, Father, reveal him to me in Jesus name.
Proverb 11: 9.

Every family member or friends who have gone to the grave and have left behind for me a curse; Lord, from today, let every of their curses return to their grave in Jesus name..
Numbers 22 :12.

Every negative word of man spoken into my

life, let the blood of Jesus erase it from my life in Jesus name.
Matthew 12:36.

Every spoken word of man troubling the journey of my life, Lord, Let the dew of heaven wash it away in Jesus name.
Genesis 30: 34.

Every myth and power of man preventing good things in my life, let the thunder from heaven strike them in Jesus name.
Genesis 6:5.

O God, send the dew of divine connection on me in Jesus name.
Luke 4:25, 26.

Every voice of man that will not allow for congratulations to be due to me this year, Father, silence it in Jesus name.
John 19:10.

Judas Iscariot identified Jesus with good pleasantries for destruction, Lord, do not

allow the wicked one to destroy my life with fake pleasantries in the name of Jesus.
Luke 22: 47.

The good things in my life that my enemies have marked for destruction, Lord hide them in Jesus name.
Luke 19:4.

Lord, send the spirit of destruction into the council that are arranging for my destruction.
Judges 9:34

Every reign of man against me prospering, tear his kingdom apart in Jesus name.
Mathew 6:10

God wants us to be fruitful

CHAPTER EIGHT

Authority Of Reproduction

Genesis 1:28 says *"And God blessed them, and God said unto them, Be fruitful, and multiply, and replenish the earth, and subdue it: and have dominion over the fish of the sea, and over the fowl of the air, and over every living thing that moveth upon the earth.*

God wants us to be fruitful here on this planet earth; hence, He commanded that we should be fruitful. Many people exist today and their lives are not fruitful. The fruitfulness I am referring is not just limited to the fruit of the womb. Our lives must be fruitful in all ramifications.

However, for your life to be fruitful, it calls for several things. Using the picture of the tree as an illustration, it is observed that the tree has many fruits because it must have been planted on the right type of soil, and well rooted in the soil. Thus, for us to be fruitful, we must be well rooted in God, the source of all things.

We can achieve this by being in constant fellowship with HIM and also being faithful in His assignments. We also need to fear God by staying away from sin and acts of wickedness. In the case of Joseph in the Bible, the fear of God was a great protection in his life, which also brought him the abundant blessings of God. There is the need for us to have a forgiving nature, fortitude and endurance because only then will the spirit of God in us give us supernatural wisdom and understanding which will help us to accomplish great things in our lives.

For us to be fruitful, we must be well rooted in God, the source of all things

Today, there are several young ladies and young men that are well over forty years and are yet unmarried. There are also several couples today who have been married for twenty years or more without any fruit of the womb and are still looking up to God in this regard. A lot of lives today are barren of good things of life. Several people struggle through life without anything to show for their existence here on planet earth.

A lot of us worked for thirty years or more, with nothing on ground to fall on after retirement. Absolutely nothing!.

Several business organizations are not growing, while some are folding up. Certainly, there are forces of darkness that are working against fruitfulness in the lives of many today. These forces may be in form of curses (family curses), and powers in the environment where we found

> There is a miracle that your life needs to give birth to, and so you need this authoritative word of multiplication

ourselves. There is also the spirit of delay manifesting in the lives of many today and spiritual wickedness in high places. Look at your own life too, and make an assessment of how fruitful you have been! There is a miracle that your life needs to give birth to, and so you need this authoritative word of multiplication to bring it about in your life. In the year 2010 Convention of the Baptist Denomination in Nigeria, at Abuja, there was the story of a 52 year old woman, who had been waiting on the Lord for the fruit of the womb and who by the mercy of God, delivered a set of twins last year 2009. There is nothing God cannot do, and according to the scriptures in the book of Luke 1:37" *For with God nothing shall be impossible,"*. May be you have not been fruitful all these years, begin now by speaking the authority of fruitfulness into your life and situation:

Songs:
I have made you too small in my eyes
Oh Lord, forgive me
And I have believed in a lie
That You were unable to help me

But now, o Lord, I see my wrong
Heal my heart and show Yourself strong,
And in my eyes and with my song
O Lord, be magnified,
O Lord, be magnified!

Prayer points:
Every spirit that is working against my fruitfulness, I bind you in the name of Jesus..
Exodus 23:26.

Lord, deliver my destiny from the stony ground of the wicked that my life is rooted preventing me from being well rooted and fruitful.
Matthew 13:6.

Every power of darkness working on how the root of my life shall be uprooted, Lord! destroy them in Jesus name.
Luke 17: 6.

Destroy every power of man that is turning the tree of my life into a bad one thus making my fruit to me bad.
Luke 6:43.

Lord, multiply me and make my life like that of the stars of heaven shining for all men can see.
Deuteronomy 1: 10.

As old as Elizabeth was, no one knew she could still conceive. Lord, don't let my miracle die in me without manifestation.
Luke 1: 24-25

Everything in my life that is hindering my being fruitful, let it be consumed by fire in Jesus name.
Genesis 17:6

Every spirit of delay like the prince of Persia, to my miracles, father, destroy it in Jesus name.
Daniel 10:13.

Every power that is killing the glory of fruitfulness in my life, let it be consumed by fire in Jesus name.
Proverb 30:16

Lord, destroy every power that is saying that I shall not be fruitful in life.
Leviticus 26:9

Every arrow of evil, barrenness and unfruitfulness that has been shot at me, father return them back to the sender in seven folds in Jesus name.
I Samuel 20:20, Psalm 11:2

I will produce glory in the name of Jesus.
Matthew 1: 21

Every hidden glory of my life, I speak to you with the authority of the word, come forth in Jesus name..
Isaiah 45:3

Where ever it has been said that I will NEVER be fruitful, Father, I call on your name today and because of your covenant and your word, let my life begin to be fruitful.
Genesis 1:22, Genesis 9:7.

If you have never experienced or done anything good since you were born on this planet earth, please pray the prayers below: lying down on the floor with your stomach on the ground saying:

I speak to the soil with the authority of God that every fruitless tree of my life be uprooted in Jesus name.
    Mark 4:7

The testimonies the world is expecting from my life; begin to show up in Jesus name.
    Romans 8:19

Before you pray the following prayers, put some soil in your hand and speak to the soil that:

Everything made from the soil that should give my life a good meaning, let my hands begin to receive it from now on in Jesus name.
Genesis 1: 24, 26.

Every dryness in my life, I speak to you that as rain falls at its season and makes the ground productive, be productive in Jesus name

Isaiah 41:18.

As the Lord spoke to the ground to bring forth good things, I speak to everything that is made of soil to bring joy and happiness to me in Jesus name.

Genesis 1: 11

Conclusion

Beloved, I urge you to be courageous and be hopeful. The Bible says in Genesis 1:31 that *"And God saw everything that he had made, and, behold, it was very good. And the evening and the morning were the sixth day"*. No matter your present situation, I assure you that in the name of our Lord Jesus Christ, you will come out of it a better person. The scripture says in Genesis 1:31 that after creation, God saw that everything He made was good. After every of your present challenges, your story will be good again in Jesus name. You will sing a new song and it shall be a song of victory. The Bible says in the book of Psalms 30: 5, *"weeping may endure for a night, but joy commeth in the morning"*. Your miracle will locate you in the name of Jesus. You are loosed by the authority of the word.

The Bible says in John 8:36 that: *"So if the Son sets you free, you are truly free"* You are set free from every oppression of the devil in Jesus name. You shall be happy again. I prophesy into your life, you will overcome by the power of the authority of the word in Jesus name. It is well with your soul in Jesus name. Amen.

For more information on how to get copies of this books:

Contact:

Pastor Oladejo, ZOA
Lord's Portion Ministries International
P. O. Box 6742, Ikeja, Lagos, Nigeria.

Email:
lordsportionministries@gmail.com
Telephone: +234 9036995904,
+234 8034739470,
+234 8029316302,
+234 8075775836.

Other Available Titles From The Lord's Portion Publishers

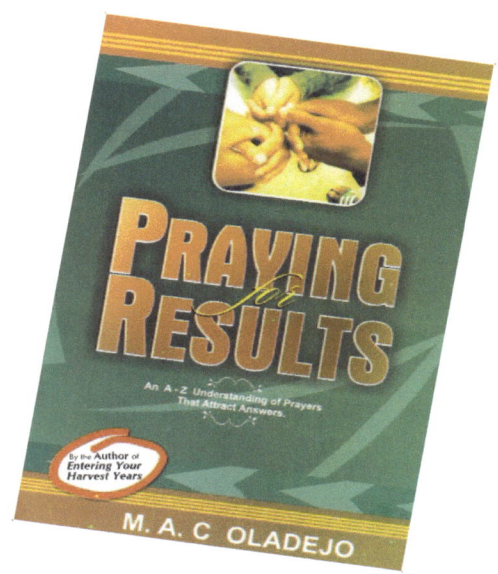

www.ingramcontent.com/pod-product-compliance
Lightning Source LLC
Chambersburg PA
CBHW042126080426
42734CB00001B/11